Cooking for Two

Kenneth Davies

Help4U Publishing

First Edition 2001

ISBN 1842740245

Internet: www.recipes4one.co.uk

Published by Help4U Publishing, Preston, UK.
http://www.help4u.net
Printed and bound in Great Britain by Antony Rowe Ltd, Eastbourne

Help4U Publishing

Acknowledgments

This book is dedicated to Christine without whom I would never of got started.

I would like to thank Jean and Kevin the proofreaders for their help and support. Not forgetting Ivy and Helen for their help in tasting the many recipes.

Introduction

Cooking for Two is a collection of recipes that have been created just for two. *Cooking for Two* is not just for those of us find the children have moved out, but also for anyone who needs to cook a meal two. All the recipes have been designed to use the basic of cooking utensils.

If you wish to try something new or find that others do not have similar tastes or preferences then this book for you. Need a cookbook over the holidays when you find you are on your own then this will fit the bill.

Like a particular recipes but find there are 4 or more of you no problem just multiply the ingredients by how many of you there it is that simply. Cooking with out kitchen scales all that is needed for these recipes is a set of measuring spoons and measuring cups..

Contents

Appetizers and Soups

Avocado Soup

2	Small	Avocados
4	Drops	Lime Juice
1		Chicken Stock Cube
4	Cups	Water
1	Teaspoon	Dry sherry
¼	Cup	Cream
1	Pinch	Salt
1	Pinch	Cayenne Pepper

1. Peel and remove the stones from the avocados.
2. Add the avocados and lemon juice into a blender and puree them.
3. Dissolve the chicken stock cube in the water and add to the blender.
4. Then add the sherry and blend for few seconds only.
5. Pour into two bowls and whisk in the cream.
6. Season to taste with salt and cayenne pepper.
7. Chill and serve.

Avocado with Crab

2	Small	Avocados
2	Teaspoons	Lemon Juice
2	Cloves	Garlic, crushed
1	Pinch	Sea Salt
1	Pinch	Freshly Ground Black Pepper, to taste
2	Pinches	Paprika
1	Cup	White Crab Meat, tinned or fresh
3	Small	Spring Onions to garnish, chopped

1. Peel and remove the stones from the avocados and mash the flesh with a fork.

2. Mix together the lemon juice, garlic and seasonings and add to the mashed avocado.

3. Flake the crabmeat and stir into the avocado mixture with a fork.

4. Divide the mixture between two plates and garnish with chopped spring onions.

Baby Pineapple Boats

2	Baby	Pineapples
1	Cup	Cottage Cheese
2	Tablespoons	Walnuts, chopped
2	Pinches	Salt & Pepper

1. Cut baby pineapples in half lengthways leaving the green top on.
2. Remove the pineapple flesh carefully to leave a boat shape.
3. Chop up the pineapple flesh discarding any core.
4. Add the cheese, salt, pepper, walnuts and the chopped pineapple to a bowl and mix.
5. Spoon back into pineapple skins and chill before serving.

Celery Soup

2	Teaspoons	Butter
4	Cups	Warm Water
1	Whole	Vegetable Stock Cube
1	Cup	Milk
4	Sticks	Celery, finely chopped
2	Small	Onions, chopped
2	Small	Potatoes, peeled and diced
1	Pinch	Salt & Pepper

1. Melt butter in a heavy saucepan over a medium heat.
2. Add celery, potatoes and onions sauté for 3 to 4 minutes
3. Dissolve the stock cube in the warm water and add to pan.
4. Stir and bring to a boil add salt and pepper.
5. Lower the heat and cover and simmer for 25 minutes then add milk.
6. Serve at once with thick crusty bread.

Cheese & Mushroom Rolls

4	Sheets	Filo Pastry
4	Tablespoons	Extra Virgin Olive Oil, warmed
1	Cup	Cheddar Cheese, chopped and skinned
2	Medium	Mushrooms, chopped
2	Teaspoons	Lime Juice
1	Teaspoon	Mixed Herbs

1. Lay the sheets of filo pastry flat and brush with oil then fold in half, length ways.

2. Mix together the mushrooms, cheese, tomatoes, limejuice and herbs.

3. Place an equal amount of the mixture across one end of each of the folded filo sheets.

4. Now start at this end and roll up the pastry.

5. Transfer to an oiled baking sheet and brush with oil.

6. Bake in a moderate oven at 375°F, 190°C or Gas Mark 5 for 12 to 18 minutes till golden brown.

7. Place two cheese and mushroom rolls on each plate and serve with a side salad.

Cheese Soufflé

1	Cup	Cheese, grated
1	Can	Condensed Chicken Soup
2	Medium	Eggs
1	Pinch	Salt & Pepper

1. Butter two small soufflé dishes.
2. Separate the eggs.
3. Empty chicken soup into a bowl and add the cheese, egg yolks, salt and pepper mix together well.
4. Now whisk the egg whites until they are stiff then fold into the yolk mixture.
5. Then pour into the dishes and bake at 400°F, 200°C or Gas Mark 6 for 20 to 25 minutes until golden brown.
6. To serve place the dishes on small plates with thinly sliced French bread.

Deep Fried Garlic Mushrooms

20	Small	Button Mushrooms
6	Cloves	Garlic, crushed
2	Cups	Flour
2	Large	Eggs
2	Cups	Fresh Breadcrumbs
2	Tablespoons	Butter

1. Wipe mushrooms with damp kitchen paper.
2. In a bowl mix the butter and garlic together.
3. Remove the stems from mushrooms and discard, now fill the mushrooms with the butter mix.
4. Then coat with flour shaking off any excess.
5. In a flat dish mix together the breadcrumbs and the seasonings.
6. In a separate bowl beat the eggs.
7. Dip the floured mushrooms in the beaten egg and then in the breadcrumbs.
8. Rest in the refrigerator for 30 minutes.
9. In oil deep-fry the coated mushrooms for about 3 to 4 minutes or until the coating is golden brown.

French Onion Soup

2	Large	Onions, sliced into rings
2	Tablespoons	Butter
1	Pinch	Salt & Pepper
2	Teaspoons	Worcestershire Sauce
1		Beef Stock Cube
½	Cup	Red Wine
4	Cups	Water
2	Cloves	Garlic, crushed
2	Slices	French Bread, thickly sliced
2	Tablespoons	Mozzarella Cheese, grated
2	Teaspoon	Parmesan Cheese

1. Melt the butter in a pan over a medium heat add the onions cover and sauté for 15 to 18 minutes until soft.

2. Remove the cover stir well and increase the heat.

3. Let the onions caramelise but keep stirring to stop them burning for about 15 to 20 minutes.

4. Dissolve the stock cube in the water.

5. Add the stock, wine, worcestershire sauce, salt and pepper.

6. Bring the liquid to the boil and then cover and reduce to a slow simmer for about 15 to 20 minutes.

7. Place bread on a baking sheet and bake in an oven at 275°F, 140°C or Gas Mark 1 for 20 to 25 minutes.

8. Ladle the soup into heatproof soup bowls, place bread on top and sprinkle with the mozzarella cheese.

9. Place under a grill until the cheese is melted serve at once.

Garlic Bread

1		Parsley and Garlic Stock Cube
2	Tablespoon	Butter
1		Baguette

1. In a small bowl mix the parsley and garlic stock cube with the butter until a smooth paste forms.
2. Cut slots in the baguette cross way but not all the way though.
3. Spread the mixture into the cut surfaces of the bread.
4. Place on a baking sheet and brush the bread lightly with water.
5. Bake in a moderate oven at 350°F, 180°C or Gas Mark 4 for 4 minutes.
6. Remove and serve at once.

Grapefruit & Stilton Surprise

1	Medium	Pink Grapefruit
2	Tablespoons	Sugar
2	Tablespoons	Port
2	Cups	Stilton, crumbled

1. Cut grapefruit in half, and with a knife loosen the segments removing any pips.

2. Place each half in an ovenproof dish.

3. Sprinkle with the sugar and cheese, then pour the port over the top.

4. Place under a hot grill for a few minutes until the cheese melts and turns brown.

5. Serve at once.

Grapefruit Surprise

1	Medium	Pink Grapefruit
2	Tablespoons	Sugar
2	Tablespoons	Port

1. Cut grapefruit in half loosen segments with a knife and remove any pips.
2. Place the halves in ovenproof dishes, sprinkle with sugar and pour the port over the top.
3. Place under a hot grill for a few minutes until the sugar melts and turns brown.
4. Remove and serve at once.

Leek & Pasta Soup

½	Cup	Macaroni, uncooked
6	Medium	Leeks, sliced
2	Medium	Potatoes, diced
2	Teaspoons	Butter
1		Vegetable Stock Cube
4	Cups	Water
1	Pinch	Salt & Pepper

1. Clean and wash the leeks under running water.
2. Peel the potatoes and diced them.
3. Cut leeks into thin slices.
4. Melt the butter in a saucepan over a medium heat.
5. Add the leeks and sauté for 4 to 5 minutes until just soft.
6. Dissolve the stock cube in the water.
7. To the saucepan add the stock, potatoes, macaroni, salt and pepper.
8. Bring the to boil and then cover and reduce to a slow simmer for about 30 to 35 minutes.

Melba Feta Cheeses

2	Cups	Feta Cheese, crumbled
1	Medium Tin	Plum Tomatoes, drained and chopped
2	Teaspoons	Chives, fresh or dried
2	Teaspoons	Basil, fresh or dried
2	Teaspoons	Oregano, fresh or dried
8	Rounds	Melba Toast
1	Pinch	Salt & Pepper

1. In small bowl, mix together the tomatoes, chives, basil, oregano, salt and pepper.
2. Spread the mixture onto the melba toast and top with the cheese.
3. Place under a moderate grill just until the cheese browns.
4. Remove from grill and serve at once.

Mushrooms Stuffed Blue Cheese

2	Large	Flat Fresh Field Mushrooms
2	Tablespoons	Butter
1	Medium	Red Pepper, finely chopped
2	Tablespoons	Double Cream
2	Tablespoons	Blue Cheese, crumbled
2	Teaspoons	Basil
1	Pinch	Ground Black Pepper

1. Wipe the mushrooms with damp kitchen paper.
2. Remove mushroom stems, finely chop stems and set aside.
3. Sauté mushroom caps in butter in frying pan until almost tender; remove from pan and drain on kitchen paper.
4. Sauté mushroom stems and the red peppers in the frying pan.
5. Add the cream and bring to the boil.
6. Reduce heat and add cheese cook until cheese is melted.
7. Stir in basil, and pepper.
8. Spoon mixture into mushroom caps.
9. Place mushroom caps in greased shallow baking pan.
10. Cover and bake in a moderate oven at 350°F, 180°C or Gas Mark 4 for 10 minutes or until tender.
11. Garnish the stuffed mushrooms with basil and serve at once.

Pears with Stilton

1	Medium Tin	Pears Halves
4	Tablespoons	Blue Cheese, crumbled
4	Teaspoons	Mayonnaise
2	Tablespoons	Milk
2	Tablespoons	Double Cream
2	Pinches	Paprika
2	Packets	Mixed Salad

1. Wash the mixed salad and drain on kitchen paper.

2. Place salad on a plate.

3. Open pears and drain and place pears cut side down on the salad.

4. In a bowl mix the cheese, mayonnaise, cream and milk.

5. Spoon over pears and sprinkle the paprika on top and serve at once.

Pineapple & Cheese Delight

2	Slices	Bread
4	Whole	Pineapple Slices, drained
2	Slices	Gouda Cheese Slices
2	Tablespoons	Butter

1. Toast bread on both sides.
2. Butter toast and top each slice of bread with a pineapple slice.
3. Then cover with the slice of gouda cheese.
4. Grill until the cheese melts and serve at once.

Potato Skins with Cajun Dip

2	Medium	Baked Potatoes
1	Cup	Natural Yoghurt
2	Teaspoons	Tomato Puree
1	Tablespoon	Cajun Spice

1. Preheat oven to 400°F, 200°C or Gas Mark 6
2. Wash the potatoes and cook for about 40 minutes or until cooked.
3. When cooked halve baked potatoes lengthwise and scoop out pulp, leaving some pulp attached to skin try to avoid breaking the skin.
4. Cut potato skins into quarters and place on grill skin-sides down grill for about 5 minutes or until crisp.
5. Mix the yoghurt and cajun spice and serve with potato skins

Prawn Soup

2	Cups	Raw Prawns, peeled
2	Small	Onions, finely chopped
2	Small	Red Bell Peppers, finely chopped
4	Cloves	Garlic, crushed
1		Fish Stock Cube
4	Cups	Hot Water
2	Tablespoons	Cold Water
2	Tablespoons	Cornflour
2	Teaspoons	Oyster Sauce
1	Pinch	Salt & Pepper

1. Melt the butter in a saucepan over a medium heat.
2. To the saucepan add the onions, chopped peppers, salt, pepper and garlic then sauté until just soft about 4 to 5 minutes.
3. Dissolve the stock cube in the hot water and add to the saucepan and stir well.
4. Now blend the cornflour with the cold water and oyster sauce add to pan.
5. Wash and clean prawns add to pan and bring to the boil.
6. Reduce the heat to low and simmer for 8 to 10 minutes until the soup thickens.
7. To serve ladle into warm soup bowls.

Tomato & Carrot Soup

1	Medium Tin	Tomatoes, chopped
2	Teaspoons	Butter
4	Medium	Carrots, peeled and diced
2	Small	Onions, chopped
4	Cups	Warm Water
1		Vegetable Stock Cube
2	Teaspoons	Basil
1	Pinch	Salt & Pepper

1. Melt the butter in a heavy saucepan over a medium heat.
2. Add the diced carrots and chopped onion and sauté for 3 to 4 minutes.
3. Now add sugar, tomatoes and basil cover and cook over low heat for 3 minutes.
4. Mix stock cube with warm water and add to saucepan.
5. Stir and bring to a boil add salt and pepper.
6. Lower the heat and cover.
7. Simmer for 35 minutes.
8. To serve ladle into warm soup bowls.

Vegetable Soup

2	Teaspoons	Butter
1	Medium Tin	Tomatoes, chopped
2	Medium	Carrots, peeled and diced
2	Small	Onions, chopped
2	Small	Potatoes, peeled and diced
1	Pinch	Salt & Pepper
1	Pinch	Sugar
1		Vegetable Stock Cube
4	Cups	Warm Water

1. Melt butter in a heavy saucepan over a medium heat.
2. Add carrots, potatoes and onions sauté for 3 to 4 minutes
3. Dissolve the stock cube in the warm water and add to pan.
4. Stir and bring to a boil add tomatoes, salt and pepper.
5. Lower the heat and cover and simmer for 35 minutes.
6. To serve ladle into warm soup bowls and serve at once with a slice of thick crusty bread.

Breakfasts

A Full Breakfast

2	Slices	Whole Wheat Bread, toasted
2	Teaspoons	Butter
4	Medium	Fresh Mushrooms, thin sliced
2	Medium	Tomatoes, thin sliced
2	Tablespoons	Parmesan Cheese, grated
2	Rashers	Smoked Bacon, chopped
2	Dashes	Worcestershire Sauce

1. Place toast on baking sheet.
2. Spread with butter if desired.
3. Cover with mushroom and tomato slices.
4. Sprinkle cheese and bacon on top and add a dash of worcestershire sauce.
5. Bake in a moderate oven at 350°F, 180°C or Gas Mark 4 until for 7 to 9 minutes till cheese melts.

Apple & Cheese Toast

2	Tablespoon	Butter
2	Medium	Red Eating Apple
2	Slice	Brown Bread
1	Teaspoon	Ground Cinnamon
4	Slices	Edam Cheese

1. Melt butter in a heavy saucepan over a medium heat.
2. Core, quarter and slice the apples.
3. Add ground cinnamon and apple to saucepan and sauté for 4 to 5 minutes.
4. Toast the bread on both sides.
5. Lay the apples on the toast and cover with cheese.
6. Place under a grill for a 3 to 4 minutes until cheese melts.

Bacon & Cheese Croissants

2		Croissants
2	Slices	Cheddar Cheese, cut half
2	Rashers	Bacon

1. Grill the bacon until it is cooked.
2. Cut each croissant in half leaving a hinged side.
3. Toast each croissant until it is a light golden brown.
4. Place open toasted croissants on plates, on one side, place the cheese halves on the other sides place the bacon.
5. Return to grill until the cheese is just melting and croissant is only lightly toasted.
6. Close together the two halves of each croissant and eat at once.

Bacon & Cheese with Garlic Croissants

2		Croissants
2	Tablespoons	Low Fat Soft Cheese with Garlic
2	Rashers	Bacon

1. Grill the bacon until it is cooked.

2. Cut the croissants in half leaving a hinged side.

3. Toast croissant until it is a light golden brown.

4. Place open toasted croissant on plates, on one side, place the cheese on the other sides place the bacon.

5. Close together the two halves of each croissant and eat at once.

Bacon & Cheese with Herbs Croissants

2		Croissants
2	Tablespoons	Low Fat Soft Cheese with Herbs
2	Rashers	Bacon

1. Grill the bacon until it is cooked.
2. Cut each croissant in half leaving a hinged side.
3. Toast croissant until it is a light golden brown.
4. Place open toasted croissant on plates, on one side, place the cheese on the other sides place the bacon.
5. Return to grill until the cheese is just melding and croissant is only lightly toasted.
6. Close together the two halves of each croissant and eat at once.

Bacon & Egg Croissants

2		Croissants
2	Teaspoons	Milk
2	Rashers	Bacon
2	Medium	Eggs
2	Teaspoons	Chives
1	Tablespoon	Butter

1. Grill the bacon until it is cooked.

2. Cut each croissant in half leaving a hinged side.

3. Break the eggs into a small jug add milk, chives and beat lightly.

4. Melt the butter in a small frying pan, over a medium heat and add the egg mixture, cook.

5. Toast each croissant until it is a light golden brown.

6. Place open toasted croissant on plates, on one side, place the eggs on the other sides place the bacon.

7. Close together the two halves of each croissant and eat at once.

Baked Eggs with Mushrooms

1	Medium Tin	Mushrooms in a Cream Sauce
4	Large	Eggs
2	Tablespoons	Butter
¼	Cup	Cheese, grated
1	Pinch	Salt & Pepper

1. Butter four ramekins dishes.
2. Divide the mushrooms in a cream sauce between the four ramekins dishes.
3. Now break an egg carefully into each dish.
4. Sprinkle with salt and pepper to taste.
5. Pour a tablespoon of cream over each egg.
6. Dot eggs with butter and sprinkle with the cheese.
7. Set the ramekins dishes into a baking tin.
8. Now add enough boiling to come half way up the out sides of the dishes.
9. Bake in a moderate oven at 350°F, 180°C or Gas Marks 8 for 10 minutes or until eggs are set.

Banana Breakfast Shake

4	Cups	Milk
2	Medium	Bananas, peeled and sliced
10		Ice Cubes
2	Teaspoon	Wheat germ
6	Drops	Vanilla Extract

1. Combine all the ingredients in blender.

2. Blend until smooth, about 30 seconds.

3. Then pour into two glasses and drink at once.

Cream Cheese Omelette with Tomato

2	Large	Eggs
2	Teaspoons	Cream Cheese
2	Teaspoons	Cream
1	Pinch	Salt & Pepper
2	Tablespoons	Butter
2	Whole	Fresh Tomatoes, peeled, seeded & chop

1. Beat the eggs until light then beat in cream, salt, and pepper.
2. Melt butter in a frying pan over a moderate heat.
3. Pour eggs into frying pan.
4. When just starting to set, but still soft, spread tomatoes and cheese over top.
5. Then fold in half and brown on both side.
6. Remove from pan and serve on a warm plate with a green side salad.

Crepes with Tuna Garlic & Herbs

3	Cups	SR Flour White
2	Cups	Milk
1	Cup	Water
2	Large	Eggs
1	Medium Tin	Tuna with Mayonnaise Garlic and Herbs
2	Cups	Cheddar Cheese, grated

1. Add the flour, milk, eggs and water to a mixing bowl and beat on high speed for 1 minute with an electric mixer or for 5 minutes with a hand balloon whisk.

2. Refrigerate mixture for 2 hours or overnight.

3. Place a small flying pan or omelette pan over a medium heat and brush the bottom and sides of pan with the oil.

4. Then pour in ¼ cup of the batter into the pan; tipping the pan to coat bottom with batter then using spatula gently pull it away from edges of the pan.

5. Cook until top is just set and bottom is lightly browned then with a spatula, turn the crepe over and cook the other side for about 1 minute remove from pan cover and keep warm.

6. Repeat the procedure until all batter is used.

7. Open the tuna and stir it then place a small amount in the centre of each crepe.

8. Fold the crepes in half then half again into quarters and place in an ovenproof dish.

9. Sprinkle the grated cheese over the top of the crepes.

10. Bake in a moderate oven at 350°F, 180°C or Gas Mark 4 for 5 minutes or until the cheese melts.

Hot Scrambled Eggs

4	Medium	Eggs
2	Small	Onions, chopped very fine
2	Tablespoons	Butter
2	Teaspoons	Tomato Puree
2	Teaspoons	Curry Powder
2	Slices	Bread

1. Place a saucepan over a moderate heat and add the butter.
2. Add the curry powder and onions cook until there are soft.
3. Break the eggs into a bowl add the tomato puree and beat well.
4. Add the egg mixture to the saucepan and stir well then reduce to a low heat.
5. Stir occasionally until eggs are set.
6. Toast bread under grill and spoon eggs on it and eat at once.

Jugged Kippers

1	Pair	Fresh Kippers
1	Large Jug	Boiling Water

1. Place the kippers in a large jug.
2. Pour the boiling water over it so the tails are just uncovered.
3. Leave for 5 minutes then remove.
4. To serve place on warm plate topped with a knob of butter.

Peach Delight

2	Cups	Peach Yoghurt
2	Cups	Canned Sliced Peaches
10	Whole	Ice Cubes
4	Cups	Milk

1. Combine all the ingredients in blender.
2. Blend until smooth, about 30 seconds.
3. Pour into two glasses and drink at once.

Pear &Cheese Toast

2	Tablespoon	Butter
2	Medium	Eating Par
1	Teaspoon	Ground Cinnamon
2	Slice	Brown Bread
4	Slices	Edam Cheese

1. Melt butter in a heavy saucepan over a med heat.
2. Core, quartered and sliced the pears
3. Add ground cinnamon and pear to saucepan and sauté for 4 to 5 minutes.
4. Toast the bread on both sides.
5. Lay pears on the toast and cover with cheese.
6. Place under a grill for a 3 to 4 minutes until cheese melts.

Pineapple Delight

2	Cups	Vanilla Yoghurt
1	Cup	Canned Pineapple Bits
10		Ice Cubes
4	Cups	Milk

1. Combine all the ingredients in blender.
2. Blend until smooth, about 30 seconds.
3. Pour into two glasses and drink at once.

Quick Kedgeree

1	Cup	Cooked White Rice
1	Cup	Cooked Smoked Haddock, flaked
2	Medium	Eggs, hard-boiled and chopped
2	Tablespoons	Evaporated Milk
2	Tablespoons	Turmeric
1	Teaspoon	Nutmeg, grated

1. Mix all the ingredients in a bowl except the oil.
2. Heat a frying pan over a moderate heat and the oil then empty the bowl into the pan and warm for about 3 to 5 minutes.
3. Place on a warm plate and eat at once.

Scottish Rarebit

2	Portions	Finnan Haddock
4	Cups	Milk
2	Tablespoons	Flour
1	Cup	Cheese, grated
2	Medium	Eggs
1	Pinch	Salt & Pepper

1. Place in a saucepan just enough salted water to cover the fish and bring to the boil.
2. Add the fish and cook for 7 minutes.
3. Remove the fish and place in an ovenproof dish.
4. Blend the flour with the milk in a bowl.
5. Place another saucepan over a moderate heat and add the milk mixture, bring to a boil then add the eggs and half the cheese.
6. Stir the mixture until sauce thickens about 3 to 4 minutes.
7. Pour over the fish and sprinkle with the rest of the cheese
8. Place under a grill to just let the cheese brown.
9. Spoon on to warm plates and eat at once.

Scrambled Egg Pockets

1	Medium Tin	Tomatoes, drained and chopped
2	Small	Onions, chopped
2	Small	Green Bell Peppers, chopped
2	Large	Eggs
2	Tablespoons	Extra Virgin Olive Oil
2	Teaspoons	Mixed Herbs
1	Pinch	Salt & Pepper
2		Garlic Pita Breads

1. Make a pocket in both pita breads by cutting down one edge.

2. Heat a frying pan and add the oil.

3. Add onions and peppers to pan and sauté for 5 to 6 minutes until softened.

4. Now add, tomatoes to pan and sauté for a further 2 minutes.

5. Then add herbs, salt and pepper to eggs and beat, now pour into frying pan and stir until set.

6. Spoon into the pita bread pockets and serve at once on to warm plates.

Smoked Haddock on Toast

2	Portions	Finnan Haddock
2	Tablespoons	Butter
2	Cups	Milk
2	Tablespoons	Flour
2	Slices	Bread, toasted
1	Pinch	Salt & Pepper

1. Add the milk and butter to saucepan, place over a moderate heat and add fish and cook for 5 to 6 minutes.
2. When cooked remove the fish and flake it into dish removing any bones or skin, keep warm.
3. Blend the flour with a little milk taken from the saucepan then add to rest of milk and stir well.
4. Bring to a boil and stir the mixture until sauce thickens about 3 to 4 minutes.
5. Toast the breads and butter them, top with the flaked fish pour sauce over the top and serve at once.

Strawberry Delight

2	Cups	Strawberry Yoghurt
2	Cups	Tinned Strawberries
4	Cups	Milk
10		Ice Cubes

1. Combine all the ingredients in blender.
2. Blend until smooth, about 30 seconds.
3. Pour into two glasses and drink at once.

Main Meals

Bacon & Cheese Pizza

2	Cups	SR Flour
4	Tablespoons	Extra Virgin Olive Oil
2	Tablespoons	Water
1	Teaspoon	Salt
1	Medium Tin	Tomatoes, chopped
2	Cups	Cheese, grated
2	Rashers	Smoked Bacon, chopped
2	Teaspoons	Italian Seasoning

1. In a bowl mix the flour, salt, water and oil to form a stiff dough.

2. Roll out the dough on a floured surface into a circle.

3. Then place onto to a greased baking sheet.

4. Heat a pan over moderate heat and add tomatoes and herbs bring to the boil and let boil for 5 to 7 minutes until the sauce has reduced by half.

5. Spoon over base and top with bacon and then the cheese.

6. Bake in a moderate oven at 400°F, 200°C or Gas Mark 6 for 15 to 20 minutes till golden brown.

7. Cut into quarters and place on warm plates and serve at once

Beef Burgundy

2	Portions	Beef Fillet Steak
2	Cups	Button Mushrooms
2	Small	Onions, thinly sliced
4	Tablespoons	Butter
2	Tablespoons	Brandy or Schnapps
½	Cup	Red Wine
1		Beef Stock Cube
1	Pinch	Salt & Pepper
2	Cups	Warm Water

1. Cut the steak into small cubes.
2. Heat a frying pan and add 2 tablespoon off the butter.
3. Add onions and sauté for 2 to 3 minutes until softened.
4. Now add mushrooms to pan and sauté them both for a further 2 minutes.
5. Remove from pan and add the remaining butter to pan add beef and sauté for about 3 to 5 minutes.
6. Carefully add the brandy to beef an ignite it; shake the pan until flames subside.
7. Return the mushrooms and onions to pan; add the wine, the stock cube and the water.
8. Cook for about 5 minute until and the ingredients are well heated.
9. Spoon on two warm plate and eat at once.

Beef Curry

2	Portions	Beef, cubed
2	Medium	Onions, chopped
4	Tablespoons	Butter
2	Cloves	Garlic, crushed
4	Tablespoons	Mild Curry Paste
3	Cups	Natural Yoghurt
2	Tablespoons	Coriander
2	Tablespoons	Sultanas
2	Teaspoons	Lime Juice
1	Pinch	Salt & Pepper

1. Heat a saucepan and melt the butter.
2. Add beef, garlic and onions sauté for 10 to 15 minutes.
3. In a bowl mix together the curry paste, yoghurt, limejuice, coriander and sultanas.
4. Pour the yoghurt mixture over the beef and heat gently for 1-2 minutes.
5. Divide between two warm plates and serve with nan bread and boiled white rice.

Beef Kebabs

2	Portions	Beef Steak, cubed
2	Medium	Green Peppers, cubed
16	Small	Button Mushrooms
4	Tablespoons	Natural Yoghurt
3	Teaspoons	Kebab Curry Paste
1	Pinch	Salt & Pepper
3	Cloves	Garlic, crushed

1. Place cubed beef in to a bowl with the peppers, mushrooms honey, yoghurt, garlic, seasoning and curry paste mix together.
2. Assemble kebab by push the beef onto skewers alternating with the peppers and mushrooms.
3. Cook under a hot grill for 12 to 14 minutes turning frequently.
4. Serve on a bed of wild rice.

Beef Lasagne

4	Sheets	No Per-Cooking Lasagne
1	Medium Tin	Tomatoes, chopped
4	Cups	Milk
4	Cups	Lean Minced Beef
4	Cloves	Garlic, crushed
2	Small	Onions, finely chopped
1	Cup	Mozzarella Cheese, grated
2	Teaspoons	Tomato Puree
2	Teaspoons	Italian Seasoning
2	Tablespoons	Butter
2	Tablespoons	Cornflour
1	Pinch	Salt & Pepper

1. Heat a frying pan over a moderate heat and add the beef stir until meat browns and separates into grains.

2. Peel and finely chop the onion and crush the garlic, add to the frying pan with the chopped tomatoes, tomato puree and Italian seasoning.

3. Cook for about 14 to 18 minutes until sauce thickens.

4. Put half of the mixture into a shallow ovenproof dish cover with two sheets of lasagne then the remaining sauces and top with two sheets of lasagne.

5. Place a saucepan over a medium heat add the butter and melt then add the cornflour and cook for 1 to 2 minutes stir all the time.

6. Slow add the milk, salt and pepper, stir well and increase the heat and cook for 4 minutes until sauce thickens.

7. Pour over the top of the last sheet of lasagne and sprinkle with the mozzarella cheese.

8. Bake in a moderate oven at 375°F, 190°C or Gas Mark 5 for 25 to 30 minutes till golden brown.

Beef Stroganoff

2	Portion	Beef Fillet Steak
2	Cups	Button Mushrooms
2	Small	Onions, thinly sliced
4	Tablespoons	Butter
2	Tablespoons	Brandy or Schnapps
½	Cup	Cream
1	Pinch	Salt & Pepper

1. Cut steak into thin strips about an inch long.
2. Heat a frying pan and add 2 tablespoon of the butter.
3. Add onions and sauté for 2 to 3 minutes until softened.
4. Now add mushrooms to pan and sauté them both for a further 2 minutes.
5. Remove from pan and add the remaining butter to pan add the beef and sauté for about 3 to 5 minutes.
6. Now add brandy to beef in pan an ignite shake pan until flames subside.
7. Return mushrooms and onions to pan and stir in cream.
8. Cook for about 1 minute until and the ingredients are well heated.
9. Divide between two warm plates and serve at once.

Chicken & Cheese Pizza

2	Cups	SR Flour
4	Tablespoons	Extra Virgin Olive Oil
2	Tablespoons	Water
2	Teaspoons	Salt
1	Medium Tin	Tomatoes, chopped
2	Cups	Cheese, grated
2	Cups	Cooked Chicken, chopped
2	Teaspoons	Italian Seasoning

1. In a bowl mix the flour, salt, water and oil to form a stiff dough.

2. Roll out the dough on a floured surface into a circle.

3. Then place onto a greased baking sheet.

4. Heat a pan over moderate heat and add tomatoes and herbs bring to the boil and let boil for 5 to 7 minutes until the sauce has reduced by half.

5. Pour over base and top with chicken and the cheese.

6. Bake in a moderate oven at 400°F, 200°C or Gas Mark 6 for 15 to 20 minutes till golden brown.

7. Cut into quarters and place on warm plates and serve at once

Chicken Stuffed with Mozzarella

2	Medium	Chicken Breasts
2	Tablespoons	Dijon Mustard
2	Cups	Breadcrumbs, fresh white
1	Cup	Mozzarella Cheese, grated
2	Teaspoons	Herbes De Provence
1	Pinch	Salt & Pepper
2	Cloves	Garlic, crushed
2	Teaspoons	Butter

1. Remove any skin from chicken and wipe with kitchen paper.
2. Place breast between two sheets of cling film and pound flat.
3. In a bowl mix together the breadcrumbs, herbs and seasoning.
4. In another bowl mix together the cheese, butter and garlic shape into long roll.
5. Place cheese roll at one end each of the flatten chicken breast and roll up.
6. Beat the egg in a bowl and brush the chicken with it coating evenly on both sides.
7. Dredge the chicken with the breadcrumb mixture.
8. Place chicken on an oiled baking sheet.
9. Bake in a moderate oven at 375°F, 190°C or Gas Mark 5 for 20 to 25 minutes until coating is golden brown.
10. Place on warm plates serve at once with jacket potatoes and a green side salad.

Chicken with Mushrooms & Whisky

2	Medium	Chicken Breasts, boned and skinned
2	Cups	Button Mushrooms
2	Small	Onions, thinly sliced
4	Tablespoons	Butter
2	Tablespoons	Whisky
½	Cup	Cream
1	Pinch	Salt & Pepper

1. Cut chicken into thin strips about an inch long.
2. Heat a frying pan and add 2 tablespoon off the butter.
3. Add onions and sauté for 2 to 3 minutes until softened.
4. Now add mushrooms to pan and sauté them both for a further 2 minutes.
5. Remove from pan add remaining butter to pan add chicken and sauté for about 3 to 5 minutes.
6. Now add whisky to chicken in pan an ignite shake pan until flames subside.
7. Return mushrooms and onions to pan and stir in cream.
8. Cook for about 1 minute until and the ingredients are well heated.
9. Serve at once on a warm plate.

Chilli Con Carne

4	Cups	Lean Minced Beef
2	Cups	Cooked Red Kidney Beans
2	Small Tin	Tomatoes, chopped
4	Cups	Water
1		Beef Stock Cube
2	Small	Onions, finely chopped
2	Teaspoons	Tomato Puree
2	Teaspoons	Chilli Powder

1. Heat a frying pan over a moderate heat and add the beef, onions stir until meat browns and separates into grains.

2. Add chopped tomatoes, tomato puree and chilli power.

3. Mix water with stock cube and add to pan.

4. Bring to the boil then cover and reduce heat to a simmer stir from time to time.

5. Simmer for about 30 to 35 minutes then add red bean and simmer for another 10 to 15 minutes.

6. To serve spoon into warm bowls and serve with warm crusty bread.

Deep Dish Mushroom & Cheese Pizza

2	Cups	SR Flour
4	Tablespoons	Extra Virgin Olive Oil
2	Tablespoons	Water
1	Pinch	Salt
1	Medium Tin	Tomatoes, chopped
2	Cups	Cheese, grated
2	Cups	Mushrooms, chopped
2	Teaspoons	Italian Seasoning

1. In a bowl mix the flour, salt, water and oil to form a stiff dough.

2. Roll out the dough on a floured surface into a circle.

3. Line the base and sides of a greased large yorkshire pudding tin.

4. Heat a pan over moderate heat and add tomatoes and herbs bring to the boil and let boil for 5 to 7 minutes until the sauce has reduced by half.

5. Pour over base and top with mushrooms and the cheese.

6. Bake in a moderate oven at 400°F, 200°C or Gas Mark 6 for 15 to 20 minutes till golden brown.

7. Cut into quarters and place on warm plates serve at once.

Dijon Chicken Breasts

2	Medium	Chicken Breasts
2	Tablespoons	Dijon Mustard
2	Cups	Breadcrumbs, fresh
2	Tablespoons	Parmesan Cheese, grated
2	Teaspoons	Herbes De Provence
1	Pinch	Salt & Pepper

1. Remove any skin from chicken and wipe with kitchen paper.
2. In a bowl mix together the breadcrumbs, herbs, cheese and seasoning.
3. Brush the chicken with the mustard coating evenly on both sides.
4. Dredge chicken with the breadcrumb mixture.
5. Place chicken on a oiled baking sheet.
6. Bake in a moderate oven at 375°F, 190°C or Gas Mark 5 for 20 to 25 minutes until coating is golden brown.
7. Divide between two warm plates and serve at once.

Fish Kebabs

2	Medium	Fish Steak, cubed
2	Medium	Red Pepper, cubed
16	Small	Button Mushrooms
4	Tablespoons	Natural Yoghurt
2	Teaspoons	Pasanda Curry Paste
1	Pinch	Salt & Pepper
4	Cloves	Garlic, crushed

1. Place cubed fish in to a bowl with the mushrooms, peppers, honey, yoghurt, garlic, seasoning and curry paste mix together.
2. Assemble kebab by push fish onto skewers alternating with the peppers and mushrooms.
3. Cook under a hot grill for 12 to 14 minutes turning frequently.
4. To serve place on a beds of cooked rice.

Grilled Lamb Chops with Tarragon Butter

2	Medium	Lamb Chops
2	Tablespoons	Extra Virgin Olive Oil
2	Tablespoons	Butter
1	Pinch	Salt & Pepper
2	Tablespoons	Tarragon

1. Trim the chops and wipe with kitchen paper.
2. Brush with the extra virgin olive oil dust with a little salt and pepper.
3. Cook under a hot grill for 6-7 minutes each side turning frequently.
4. Add the butter to a bowl and mix with a wooden spoon.
5. Add the tarragon and mix well in.
6. Just before serving place a large spoonful of tarragon butter on each of the chops.

Honey Turkey Breasts

2	Medium	Turkey Breasts
2	Tablespoons	Honey
2	Cups	Breadcrumbs, fresh
2	Tablespoons	Parmesan Cheese, grated
2	Teaspoons	Herbes De Provence
2	Pinches	Salt & Pepper

1. Remove any skin from turkey and wipe with kitchen paper.
2. In a bowl mix together the breadcrumbs, herbs, cheese and seasoning.
3. Brush the chicken with the honey coating evenly on both sides.
4. Dredge turkey with the breadcrumb mixture.
5. Place chicken on a oiled baking sheet.
6. Bake in a moderate oven at 375°F, 190°C or Gas Mark 5 for 20 to 25 minutes until coating is golden brown.

Lamb Chops with Port

2	Medium	Lamb Chops
2	Cups	Button Mushrooms
2	Small	Onion, sliced
2	Tablespoons	Butter
½	Small	Port
1		Chicken Stock Cube
1	Cup	Warm Water
2	Pinches	Salt & Pepper

1. Trim the chops and wipe with kitchen paper.

2. Heat a frying pan and add 1the butter.

3. Add onions and sauté for 2 to 3 minutes until softened.

4. Now add mushrooms to pan and sauté them both for a further 2 minutes.

5. Remove from pan and add remaining butter to pan and melt.

6. Add chop and sauté for about 3 to 5 minutes.

7. Now add port to chop in pan return mushrooms and onions to pan and stir in black currant jam.

8. Cook for about 10 minutes until and the ingredients thicken.

9. Serve at once on a warm plate.

Plaice with Cheese Sauce

2	Fillets	Plaice
4	Cups	Milk
4	Cloves	Garlic, chopped
4	Tablespoons	Strong Cooking Cheese, grated
4	Tablespoons	Mozzarella Cheese, grated
2	Teaspoons	Italian Seasoning
2	Tablespoons	Butter
2	Tablespoons	Cornflour
2	Pinches	Salt & Pepper

1. Place a saucepan over a medium heat add the butter and melt then add the cornflour and cook for 1 to 2 minutes stir all the time.

2. Slow add the milk, salt, pepper and cheese stir well and increase the heat and cook for 4 minutes until sauce thickens.

3. Place the fish into an ovenproof dish pour over the sauce and sprinkle with the Mozzarella Cheese.

4. Bake in a moderate oven at 375°F, 190°C or Gas Mark 5 for 18 to 20 minutes till golden brown.

Pork Chops with Sweet Potato

2	Medium	Pork Chops
2	Tablespoons	Extra Virgin Olive Oil
2	Pinches	Salt & Pepper
2	Small	Sweet Potatoes, cubed
2	Cups	Orange Juice
2	Small	Onion, very finely chopped
2	Tablespoons	Brown Sugar
2	Tablespoons	Balsamic Vinegar

1. Trim the chop and wipe with kitchen paper.
2. Heat oil in a frying pan over medium-high heat.
3. Add the pork chop and cook for 2 minutes on each side.
4. Remove chops from pan set and keep warm.
5. Now add the sweet potato and onion to pan and sauté for 4 minutes or until tender.
6. Add the orange juice, sugar and vinegar stir well.
7. Return chops to the pan cover and reduce heat.
8. Simmer for 30 to 35 or until chops are tender.
9. To serve place chop on a warm plate and pour over the sauce.

Provençal Cod

2	Portions	Cod Fillet
2	Small	Onions, finely chopped
2	Tablespoons	Extra Virgin Olive Oil
5	Cloves	Garlic, crushed
1	Medium Tin	Tomatoes, chopped
2	Teaspoons	Tomato Puree
1	Pinch	Salt & Pepper
2	Small	Yellow Pepper, chopped

1. Heat a frying pan over a moderate heat and add the oil then garlic and onion cook for 3 minutes until soft.

2. Then add pepper to pan and cook for another 2 minutes.

3. Stir in the tomatoes, salt, pepper and purée then bring to the boil and cook rapidly for 6 minutes.

4. Reduce the heat and add the fish cook slowly for 4 to 5 until fish is cooked.

5. Serve on a bed of cooked rice.

Turkey Kiev

2	Medium	Turkey Breasts
2	Tablespoons	Dijon Mustard
2	Cups	Breadcrumbs, fresh white
4	Tablespoons	Ricotta Cheese
2	Teaspoons	Herbes De Provence
1	Pinch	Salt & Pepper
2	Cloves	Garlic, crushed
2	Teaspoons	Butter

1. Remove any skin from turkey and wipe with kitchen paper.
2. Place breast between two sheets of cling film and pound flat.
3. In a bowl mix together the breadcrumbs, herbs and seasoning.
4. In a bowl mix together the ricotta cheese, butter and garlic shape into long roll.
5. Place cheese roll at one end of flatten chicken breast and roll up.
6. Beat the egg in a bowl and brush the chicken with it coating evenly on both sides.
7. Dredge turkey with the breadcrumb mixture.
8. Place chicken on an oiled baking sheet.
9. Bake in a moderate oven at 375°F, 190°C or Gas Mark 5 for 20 to 25 minutes until coating is golden brown.

Puddings

Almond Chocolate Mousse

2	Small Bars	Dark Chocolate
2	Small	Eggs
2	Tablespoons	Sugar
2	Tablespoons	Blanched Almonds, toasted & chopped
2	Teaspoons	Almond Extract

1. Break eggs and separate the yolks from whites.
2. Place whites into a clean medium sized bowl.
3. Place chocolate; egg yolks, boiling water and flavouring into a blender and blend for few seconds until chocolate is melted.
4. Now beat egg whites until foamy then gradually add the sugar and continue beating until stiff.
5. Fold chocolate mixture into egg whites until no streaks of egg white remain.
6. Turn into a ramekin dish, and chill for several hours until firm.
7. Decorate with the toasted almonds before serving.

Apple & Cheese Crumble

2	Large	Cooking Apples
1	Teaspoon	Ground Cinnamon
1	Tablespoon	Brown Sugar
½	Cup	Cheddar Cheese, grated
2	Tablespoons	SR Flour
2	Tablespoons	Rolled Oats
2	Tablespoons	Butter, cut into small pieces

1. Preheat oven to 190s°C 375s°F, 190s C or Gas Mark 5.
2. Grease a large ramekin dish.
3. Peel and core the apple and cut into pieces.
4. Mix together the apple, cinnamon, and 1 teaspoons of the brown sugar
5. Place in ramekin dish.
6. In a small bowl, mixes cheese, flour, oats, and the other teaspoon of sugar then add butter.
7. Combine the mixture together with your fingers until it resembles beard crumbs.
8. Cover apple with the crumble mixture.
9. Bake until apples are tender and topping is light brown about 25 to 30 minutes.
10. To serve pour over a little custard or drizzle with fresh cream.

Baked Alaska

½	Cup	White SR Flour
2	Small	Eggs
4	Tablespoons	Butter
½	Teaspoon	Cream of Tartar
2	Teaspoons	Water
6	Drops	Vanilla Extract
¼	Cup	Sugar
2	Tablespoons	Strawberry Jam
2	Portion	Strawberry Ice Cream

1. Cream the butter and sugar together in a medium bowl until very pale in colour, add flour, egg yolks, water and vanilla extract, beat again until smooth and creamy.

2. Grease a small cake tin and line the bottom and sides with greaseproof paper.

3. Pour the sponge mixture into prepared tin and cook in a moderate oven at 350°F, 180°C or Gas Mark 4, for 8 to 10 minutes or until golden brown and firm to the touch.

4. Remove from the oven and turn on to a wire rack to cool, after a few minutes remove the paper.

5. For the meringue, put the egg whites in to a clean dry bowl and add cream of tartar, beat well then gradually add sugar, beating until stiff peaks form.

6. Place cake, bottom side up, on an ovenproof platter and spread with the strawberry jam, add the portions of strawberry ice cream, spread the meringue over ice cream and around the sides of cake.

7. Bake in a hot oven at 450°F, 230°C or Gas Mark 8 for 2 minutes until golden brown.

8. Remove from the oven and serve at once.

Baked Apple with Whisky

2	Large	Cooking Apples
½	Cup	Glacé Cherries
2	Tablespoons	Brown Sugar
1	Teaspoon	Ground Cinnamon
1	Teaspoon	Lemon Rind, grated
2	Teaspoons	Honey
2	Tablespoons	Whisky
4	Cups	Hot Water

1. Combine glacé cherries, brown sugar, cinnamon, lemon rind, and whisky in a small bowl.
2. Core apples three quarters of the way through being careful not to cut through the bottom.
3. Place in a small baking dish.
4. Fill centre of apples with the mixture.
5. Drizzle honey over top of apple.
6. Pour the water into baking dish.
7. During cooking basting the apple with syrup from dish.
8. Bake in a preheated oven at 400°F, 200°C or Gas Mark 6 for 40 minutes or until tender.

Serving Suggestion
Pour over syrup or try serving with little custard or drizzle with fresh cream

Baked Lemon Pudding

½	Cup	SR Flour White
4	Tablespoons	Soft Butter
¼	Cup	Sugar
2		Egg Yolks
2	Tablespoons	Fresh Lemon Juice
2	Teaspoons	Lemon Rind, grated

1. Cream the butter and sugar together in a medium bowl until very pale in colour.
2. Add flour, egg yolk, lemon rind, lemon juice, and beat again until smooth and creamy.
3. Grease tin and line with bottom and side with greaseproof paper.
4. Pour Sponge mixture into prepared tin and cook in a moderate oven at 350°F, 180°C or Gas Mark 4.
5. For 8 to 10 minutes or until golden brown and firm to the touch.
6. Serve warm with a little custard or drizzle with fresh cream.

Banana Pudding

1	Cup	Milk
2	Small	Egg Yolks
2	Tablespoons	Cream
2	Teaspoons	Cornflour
2	Pinches	Salt
2	Slices	Banana, riper
6	Drops	Vanilla Extract
8	Small	Vanilla Wafers

1. Place the milk, egg yolk, cornflour and the vanilla extract in a saucepan and stir well.
2. Place over medium heat and simmer for about 7 minutes or until smooth and thickened, stirring constantly.
3. Remove from heat; stir in banana and mix well.
4. Arrange the 8 wafers around the side of a small dish then pour in the mixture.
5. Cover with plastic wrap; chill at least 2 hours.

Blackberry Soufflés

1	Medium Tin	Blackberries in Syrup
2	Teaspoons	Sugar
2	Medium	Eggs
2	Tablespoons	Butter
2	Tablespoons	SR Flour

1. Place a saucepan over a low heat add the butter and melt with a wooden spoon stir in the flour and cook for 2 minutes.

2. Now slowly add the fruit to the saucepan stir with a whisk until the sauce thickens then bring to the boil and simmer for 2 to 3 minutes.

3. Stir in the sugar and let cool.

4. Separate the egg and beat the yolk into the sauce mixture.

5. Then whisk the egg white until it is stiff and fold into sauce mixture.

6. Spoon the mixture into a buttered ramekin dish and bake at 400°F, 200°C or Gas Mark 6 for 15 to 20 minutes until golden brown.

Bread & Butter Pudding with Honey

6	Slices	Thick Sliced Bread
2	Cups	Evaporated Milk
2		Eggs
2	Tablespoons	Butter
½	Cup	Raisins
2	Tablespoons	Honey
2	Tablespoons	Sugar

1. Spread the bread with the butter and the homey.
2. Cut into quarters and place in a small ovenproof dish.
3. Mix together the milk, egg, and sugar.
4. Pour over bread and let soak for a few minutes.
5. Bake in a moderate oven at 350°F, 180°C or Gas Mark 4 for about 35 to 40 minutes.
6. Serve at once.

Bread & Butter Pudding

6	Slices	Thick Sliced Bread
2	Cups	Evaporated Milk
2		Eggs
2	Tablespoons	Butter
½	Cup	Raisins
2	Tablespoons	Mixed Dried Fruit
2	Tablespoons	Sugar

1. Spread the bread with the butter.
2. Cut into quarters and place in a small ovenproof dish.
3. Sprinkle the mixed dried fruit over the bread.
4. Mix together the milk, eggs, and sugar.
5. Pour over bread and let soak for a few minutes.
6. Bake in a moderate oven at 350°F, 180°C or Gas Mark 4 for about 35 to 40 minutes.
7. Serve at once.

Cherry Cheesecake

1	Cup	Cottage Cheese
½	Small Can	Cherry Pie filling
½	Cup	Double Cream
2	Teaspoons	Sugar
2	Teaspoons	Lemon Juice
4	Teaspoons	Soft Butter
6	Whole	Digestive Biscuits

1. In a bowl crush the digestive biscuits and add the soft butter and mix well.
2. Cover a small plate with a sheet of cling film, place a muffin ring on it.
3. Fill with the biscuit mix to cover the base push down hard with the back of a spoon.
4. Rub the cheese through a sieve into a bowl and add lemon juice mix well.
5. Whip the cream until thick and fold into the cheese mix.
6. Put cheese mix into muffin ring level top, Spread the pie filling over and chill for an hour before serving.

Chocolate Egg Custard

2	Cups	Milk
2	Medium	Eggs, beaten
4	Tablespoons	Chocolate
2	Tablespoons	Sugar
2	Teaspoons	Vanilla
1	Tablespoon	Nutmeg

1. Warm the milk in a saucepan add the chocolate and melt.
2. Break the eggs into bowl and add the vanilla and sugar then whisk together.
3. Pour hot milk into the egg mixture whisking all the time.
4. Pour the custard mixture into two ramekin dishes sprinkle with nutmeg.
5. Set the ramekin dishes into a baking tin.
6. Now add enough boiling to come half way up the sides of the dishes.
7. Bake in a moderate oven at 325°F, 160°C or Gas Mark 3 20 to 25 minutes.

Chocolate Steam Pudding

?	Cup	SR Flour
½	Cup	Caster Sugar
4	Tablespoons	Butter
4	Tablespoons	Milk
2	Medium	Eggs
2	Tablespoons	Cocoa Powder
2	Tablespoons	Sultanas or Currants or Raisins
2	Pinches	Salt

1. Sift flour and salt into a bowl.
2. Cream butter and sugar until light and fluffy.
3. Beat in the eggs, milk and add cocoa powder.
4. Then the flour a little at a time.
5. Butter a small pudding basin.
6. Put mix into basin and cover securely with tin foil.
7. Place in a steamer for 20 to 25 minutes or until firm.
8. Turn out on to a plate and serve.

Egg Custard

2	Cups	Milk
2	Medium	Eggs, beaten
2	Teaspoons	Vanilla
2	Tablespoons	Sugar
2	Pinches	Nutmeg

1. Warm the milk in a saucepan.
2. Break the eggs into bowl add the vanilla and sugar then whisk together.
3. Pour hot milk into the egg mixture whisking all the time.
4. Pour the custard mixture into two ramekin dishes sprinkle with nutmeg.
5. Set the ramekin dishes into a baking tin.
6. Now add enough boiling to come half way up the sides of the dishes.
7. Bake in a moderate oven at 325°F, 160°C or Gas Mark 3 20 to 25 minutes.

Fruit Steam Pudding

?	Cup	SR Flour
½	Cup	Caster Sugar
4	Tablespoons	Butter
4	Tablespoons	Milk
2	Medium	Eggs
2	Tablespoons	Sultanas or Currants or Raisins
2	Pinches	Salt

1. Sift flour and salt into a bowl.
2. Cream butter and sugar until light and fluffy.
3. Beat in the eggs, milk and add fruit.
4. Then the flour a little at a time.
5. Butter a small pudding basin.
6. Put mix into basin and cover securely with tin foil.
7. Place in a steamer for 20 to 25 minutes or until firm.
8. Turn out on to a plate and serve.

Orange Egg Custard

2	Cups	Milk
2	Medium	Eggs, beaten
2	Tablespoons	Orange Marmalade Fine Cut
2	Tablespoons	Sugar
2	Teaspoons	Vanilla
2	Tablespoons	Nutmeg

1. Warm the milk in a saucepan.
2. Break the eggs into a bowl add the vanilla, marmalade and sugar then whisk together.
3. Pour hot milk into the egg mixture whisking all the time.
4. Pour the custard mixture into two ramekin dishes sprinkle with nutmeg.
5. Set the ramekin dishes into a baking tin.
6. Now add enough boiling to come half way up the sides of the dishes.
7. Bake in a moderate oven at 325°F, 160°C or Gas Mark 3 20 to 25 minutes.

Orange Soufflés

2	Large	Oranges
4	Tablespoons	Sugar
2	Medium	Eggs
2	Tablespoons	Butter
2	Tablespoons	SR Flour White
2	Tablespoons	Lemon Juice

1. Wash the oranges and cut in half crossways.
2. Scoop out the flesh and remove the white pith set a shell aside.
3. Now squeeze the oranges flesh to extract all the juice and strain it into a bowl add lemon juice.
4. Place a saucepan over a low heat add the butter and melt with a wooden spoon stir in the flour and cook for 2 minutes.
5. Now slowly add the juice to the saucepan stir with a whisk until the sauce thickens then bring to the boil and simmer for 2 to 3 minutes.
6. Stir in the sugar and let cool.
7. Separate the eggs and beat the yolks into the sauce mixture.
8. Then whisk the egg whites until stiff and fold into sauce mixture.
9. Spoon the mixture into the orange shell and place into a baking tin.
10. Now add enough boiling to come half way up the sides of the shell.
11. Bake in a moderate oven at 400°F, 200°C or Gas Mark 6 for 15 to 20 minutes.

Pink Grapefruit Soufflés

2	Medium	Pink Grapefruits
4	Tablespoons	Brown Sugar
2	Medium	Eggs
2	Tablespoons	Butter
2	Tablespoons	SR Flour

1. Wash the grapefruit and cut in half crossways.
2. Scoop out the flesh and remove the white pith set a shell aside.
3. Now squeeze the grapefruit flesh to extract all the juice and strain it into a bowl.
4. Place a saucepan over a low heat add the butter and melt with a wooden spoon stir in the flour and cook for 2 minutes.
5. Now slowly add the juice to the saucepan stir with a whisk until the sauce thickens then bring to the boil and simmer for 2 to 3 minutes.
6. Stir in the sugar and let cool.
7. Separate the eggs and beat the yolks into the sauce mixture.
8. Then whisk the egg whites until stiff and fold into sauce mixture.
9. Spoon the mixture into the grapefruit shells and place into a baking tin.
10. Now add enough boiling to come half way up the sides of the shell.
11. Bake in a moderate oven at 400°F, 200°C or Gas Mark 6 for 15 to 20 minutes.

Raspberry Soufflés

1	Tin	Raspberries in Syrup
2	Teaspoons	Sugar
2	Medium	Eggs
2	Tablespoons	Butter
2	Tablespoons	SR Flour White

1. Place a saucepan over a low heat add the butter and melt with a wooden spoon stir in the flour and cook for 2 minutes.

2. Now slowly add the fruit to the saucepan stir with a whisk until the sauce thickens then bring to the boil and simmer for 2 to 3 minutes.

3. Stir in the sugar and let cool.

4. Separate the eggs and beat the yolks into the sauce mixture.

5. Then whisk the egg whites until stiff and fold into sauce mixture.

6. Spoon the mixture into a buttered ramekin dish and bake at 400°F, 200°C or Gas Mark 6 for 15 to 20 minutes until golden brown.

Spiced Peach Crumble

2	Large	Peaches
2	Teaspoons	Ground Cinnamon
1	Teaspoon	Allspice
4	Teaspoons	Brown Sugar
2	Tablespoons	SR Flour
2	Tablespoons	Rolled Oats
2	Tablespoons	Butter, cut into small pieces

1. Preheat oven to 375°F, 190°C or Gas Mark 5.
2. Grease a large ramekin dish.
3. Peel and stoned and sliced the peach.
4. Mix together the peach, ½ teaspoon of cinnamon, and 1 teaspoons of the brown sugar.
5. Place in ramekin dish.
6. In a small bowl, mix the flour, the other ½ teaspoon of cinnamon, allspice, oats, and the other teaspoon of sugar then add butter.
7. Combine the mixture together with your fingers until it resembles breadcrumbs.
8. Cover peaches with the crumble mixture.
9. Bake until peaches are tender and topping is light brown about 25 to 30 minutes.
10. To serve pour over a little custard or drizzle with fresh cream.

Summer Fruits Soufflés

1	Tin	Summer Fruits in Syrup
2	Teaspoons	Sugar
2	Medium	Eggs
2	Tablespoons	Butter
2	Tablespoons	SR Flour White

1. Place a saucepan over a low heat add the butter and melt with a wooden spoon stir in the flour and cook for 2 minutes.

2. Now slowly add the fruit to the saucepan stir with a whisk until the sauce thickens then bring to the boil and simmer for 2 to 3 minutes.

3. Stir in the sugar and let cool.

4. Separate the eggs and beat the yolks into the sauce mixture.

5. Then whisk the egg whites until stiff and fold into sauce mixture.

6. Spoon the mixture into a buttered ramekin dish and bake at 400°F, 200°C or Gas Mark 6 for 15 to 20 minutes until golden brown.

Snacks and Suppers

Beef Burgers

4	Cups	Lean Minced Beef
2	Cups	Breadcrumbs, fresh
2	Small	Onions, finely chopped
2	Teaspoons	Mix Herbs
2	Teaspoons	Tomato Puree

1. In a bowl nix together the onion, beef, breadcrumbs, herbs and tomato puree.
2. Divide the mixture to make two burgers.
3. Grill or frying burgers 10 to 12 minutes turning once.
4. Serve with relish and salad in burger buns.

Broccoli Lasagne

8	Sheets	Lasagne
1	Cup	Creamed Cottage Cheese
4	Cups	Frozen Broccoli
1	Cup	Natural Yoghurt
½	Cup	Mozzarella Cheese, grated
2	Tablespoons	Yoghurt
2	Pinches	Salt & Pepper

1. Place broccoli into a pan of boiling water and cook for 5 minutes and then drain.
2. Mix cottage cheese natural yoghurt, salt and pepper in a bowl then add the broccoli.
3. In an ovenproof dish place a quarter of the broccoli mix then cover with one sheet of lasagne
4. Repeat this twice.
5. Now add last of mix and sprinkle with the mozzarella cheese.
6. Cover tightly with aluminium foil bake in a moderate oven at 350°F, 180°C or Gas Mark 4, for 30 minutes or until cheese melts and is golden on top.

Cauliflower Casserole

4	Cups	Cauliflower Flowerets
2	Small	Eggs
2	Small	Potatoes, peeled and chopped
2	Tablespoons	Butter
1	Cup	Emmenthal Cheese, grated
2	Tablespoons	Mozzarella Cheese, grated
2	Pinches	Salt & Pepper

1. Put the potatoes and cauliflower in a pot boiling salted water and cook for 15 minutes.
2. Drain the potatoes and cauliflower and empty into a bowl.
3. Add the butter, salt and pepper and mash with a potato masher.
4. Beat the eggs and add to the bowl then stir in the emmenthal cheese.
5. Spoon into a greased ovenproof dish sprinkle with mozzarella cheese and cover.
6. Bake in a moderate oven at 350°F, 180°C or Gas Mark 4 for 20 to 25 minutes.

Cheese & Mushroom Pizza

2	Cups	SR Flour
4	Tablespoons	Extra Virgin Olive Oil
2	Tablespoons	Water
2	Teaspoons	Salt
1	Medium Tin	Tomatoes, chopped
2	Teaspoons	Italian Seasoning
2	Cups	Cheese, grated
2	Cups	Mushrooms, chopped

1. In a bowl mix the flour, salt, water and oil to a stiff dough.
2. Roll out the dough on a floured surface into a circle.
3. Then place onto a greased baking.
4. Heat a pan over moderate heat and add tomatoes and herbs bring to the boil and let boil for 5 to 7 minutes until the sauce has reduced by half.
5. Pour over base and top with mushrooms and the cheese.
6. Bake in a moderate oven at 400°F, 200°C or Gas Mark 6 for 15 to 20 minutes till golden brown

Chicken Kiev

2	Medium	Chicken Breasts
2	Tablespoons	Dijon Mustard
2	Cups	Breadcrumbs, fresh white
4	Tablespoons	Ricotta Cheese
2	Teaspoons	Herbes De Provence
1	Pinch	Salt & Pepper
2	Cloves	Garlic, crushed
2	Teaspoons	Butter

1. Remove any skin from chicken and wipe with kitchen paper.
2. Place chicken between two sheets of cling film and pound flat.
3. In a bowl mix together the breadcrumbs, herbs and seasoning.
4. In another bowl mix together the ricotta cheese, butter and garlic shape into long roll.
5. Place cheese roll at one end of flatten chicken and roll up.
6. Beat the egg in a bowl and brush the chicken with it coating evenly n both sides.
7. Dredge chicken with the breadcrumb mixture.
8. Place chicken on an oiled baking sheet.
9. Bake in a moderate oven at 375°F, 190°C or Gas Mark 5 for 20 to 25 minutes until coating is golden brown.

Chicken Risotto

2	Cups	Cooked Chicken, cut into strips
1	Cup	Italian Risotto Rice, uncooked
4	Cups	Water
2	Small	Tomatoes, chopped
2	Small	Onions, very finely chopped
2	Medium	Yellow Peppers, chopped
2		Chicken Stock Cubes
2	Tablespoons	Extra Virgin Olive Oil
1	Teaspoon	Salt & Pepper

1. Heat a saucepan and melt the butter.
2. Add onions, peppers and sauté for 2 to 3 minutes until softened.
3. Now add herbs and rice to pan stir well and cook for another 1 minute.
4. Mix stock cubes with water.
5. Add the stock, tomato, turkey, salt and pepper to the pan and bring to the boil.
6. Reduce the heat and simmer for 12 to 15 minutes until all the water has been absorbed and the rice is cooked.

Chocolate Marshmallow Popcorn

½	Cup	Un-popped Popcorn
4	Tablespoons	Butter
2	Teaspoons	Sugar
2	Tablespoons	Chocolate Chips
4	Tablespoons	Mini Marshmallows

1. Pop the popcorn in a heavy pan over a moderate heat or in a popcorn machine.
2. Melt the butter, Chocolate Chips and sugar in a saucepan over a moderate.
3. Place popcorn in a large plastic food bag.
4. Pour the butter mixture on top close the top of bag and shake well.
5. Add the mini marshmallows and close the top of bag and shake well.
6. Then empty into a bowl.

Eggs Florentine

2	Cups	Frozen Spinach, chopped
2	Large	Eggs
4	Tablespoons	Mayonnaise
2	Tablespoons	Parmesan Cheese, grated

1. Half fill a medium pan with water and put over medium heat add vinegar and bring to the boil.
2. Beak egg into a saucer and slip into boiling water.
3. Reduce the heat so water is just simmering poach for 3 to 4 minutes.
4. Cook spinach according to package directions and then drain thoroughly place on doubled kitchen paper and squeeze out as much moisture as possible.
5. Butter a ovenproof dish and place the spinach on it.
6. Place the poached egg on top of spinach and pour mayonnaise over then sprinkle it with cheese.
7. Place under a moderate grill for 5-10 minutes or until top is browned.

Fish Curry

2	Medium	Cod Fillets, cubed
2	Medium	Onions, chopped
4	Tablespoons	Butter
3	Cloves	Garlic, crushed
4	Tablespoons	Hot Curry Paste
4	Cups	Natural Yoghurt
2	Tablespoons	Coriander
2	Tablespoons	Sultanas
2	Teaspoons	Lime Juice
1	Pinch	Salt & Pepper

1. Heat a saucepan and melt the butter.
2. Add fish, garlic and onions sauté for 10 to 15 minutes.
3. In a bowl mix together the curry paste, yoghurt, limejuice, coriander and sultanas.
4. Pour the yoghurt mixture over the fish and heat gently for 1-2 minutes.
5. Serve with rice.

Garlic & Parmesan Popcorn

½	Cup	Un-popped Popcorn
2	Tablespoons	Butter
4	Teaspoons	Parmesan Cheese
2	Tablespoons	Garlic powder
2	Pinches	Salt

1. Pop the popcorn in a heavy pan over a moderate heat or in a popcorn machine.
2. Melt the butter in a saucepan over a moderate.
3. Place popcorn in a large plastic food bag.
4. Add the Parmesan cheese and garlic pour to the popcorn close the top of bag and add shake well.
5. Pour the butter mixture on top close the top of bag and again shake well.
6. Then empty into a bowl and add salt to taste.

.

Italian Lamb Strudel

1	Medium Tin	Tomatoes, chopped
4	Cups	Lean Minced Lamb
4	Sheets	Filo Pastry
4	Cloves	Garlic, crushed
2	Small	Onions, finely chopped
4	Tablespoons	Mozzarella Cheese, grated
2	Teaspoons	Tomato Puree
2	Teaspoons	Italian Seasoning
2	Tablespoons	Butter
2	Tablespoons	Extra Virgin Olive Oil
2	Pinches	Salt & Pepper

1. Heat a frying pan over a moderate heat add beef, onions and garlic stir until meat browns and separates into grains.
2. Add chopped tomatoes, tomato puree and Italian seasoning.
3. Bring to the boil then reduce heat stir from time to time.
4. Cook for about 14 to 18 minutes until sauce thickens.
5. Lay flat one of the sheets of filo pastry and brush with oil then sprinkle with the mozzarella cheese
6. Now brush the other sheet with oil and place over the top of the cheese.
7. Spread the sauce mixture over the pastry leaving a gap all around the edges.
8. Fold in the short end and roll up.
9. Transfer to an oiled baking sheet
10. Bake in a moderate oven at 375°F, 190°C or Gas Mark 5 for 15 to 20 minutes till golden brown.

Lamb Curry

2	Medium	Lamb Steaks, cubed
2	Medium	Onions, chopped
4	Tablespoons	Butter
2	Cloves	Garlic, crushed
4	Tablespoons	Mild Curry Paste
3	Cups	Natural Yoghurt
2	Tablespoons	Coriander
2	Tablespoons	Sultanas
2	Teaspoons	Lime Juice
1	Pinch	Salt & Pepper

1. Heat a saucepan and melt the butter.
2. Add lamb, garlic and onions sauté for 10 to 15 minutes.
3. In a bowl mix together the curry paste, yoghurt, lime juice, coriander and sultanas.
4. Pour the yoghurt mixture over the lamb and heat gently for 1-2 minutes.
5. Serve with rice.

Lamb Lasagne

4	Sheets	No Per-Cooking Lasagne
4	Cups	Lean Minced Lamb
4	Cups	Milk
4	Cloves	Garlic, crushed
1	Medium Tin	Tomatoes, chopped
2	Small	Onions, finely chopped
4	Tablespoons	Mozzarella Cheese, grated
2	Teaspoons	Tomato Puree
2	Teaspoons	Italian Seasoning
1	Pinch	Salt & Pepper
2	Tablespoons	Cornflour

1. Heat a frying pan over a moderate heat add beef, onions and garlic stir until meat browns and separates into grains.

2. Add chopped tomatoes, tomato puree and Italian seasoning.

3. Bring to the boil then reduce heat stir from time to time.

4. Cook for about 14 to 18 minutes until sauce thickens.

5. Put half of the mixture into a shallow ovenproof dish cover with a sheet of lasagne then the remaining sauces and top with a sheet of lasagne.

6. Place a saucepan over a medium heat add the butter and melt then add the cornflour and cook for 1 to 2 minutes stir all the time.

7. Slow add the milk, salt and pepper, stir well and increase the heat and cook for 4 minutes until sauce thickens.

8. Pour over the top of the last sheet of lasagne and sprinkle with the Mozzarella Cheese.

9. Bake in a moderate oven at 375°F, 190°C or Gas Mark 5 for 25 to 30 minutes till golden brown.

Macaroni Cheese

1	Cup	Quick-Cook Macaroni
2	Tablespoons	Butter
1	Cup	Cheddar Cheese, grated
2	Dashes	Worcestershire sauce

1. Cook macaroni according to package instructions.
2. Drain and return to pot.
3. Add butter and stir until melted over a low heat.
4. Then add cheese, stirring it constantly, until cheese melts.
5. Season with a dash of worcestershire sauce.
6. Serve at once.

Mushroom Soufflés

1	Small Tin	Mushrooms, sliced
1	Small Tin	Condensed Mushroom Soup
2	Large	Eggs
2	Pinches	Salt & Pepper

1. Greased small soufflé dish and empty in the mushrooms
2. Separate the eggs.
3. Empty the mushroom soup into a bowl and add the egg yolks, salt and pepper and mix together well.
4. Then whisk the egg whites until stiff fold into egg yolk mixture.
5. Pour over mushrooms and bake at 400°F, 200°C or Gas Mark 6 for 20 to 25 minutes until golden brown.

Prawn and Pineapple Salad

2	Cups	Cooked Peeled Prawns
2	Cups	Mayonnaise with Garlic
1	Medium Tin	Pineapple Bits, drained
1	Medium Tin	Lychees, drained
4	Sticks	Celery, finely chopped
2	Teaspoons	Clear Honey
½	Teaspoon	Chilli Powder
1	Bag	Mixed Green Salad

1. In a bowl mix the prawns, pineapples, celery and lychees

2. Add the mayonnaise, honey, soy sauces, and chilli power stir well.

3. Check mixed green salad and place on a plate spoon over the prawn mix.

4. Serve with a slice of butter brown bread.

Salmon Parcels

2	Portions	Salmon fillets
4	Sheets	Filo Pastry
4	Tablespoons	Extra Virgin Olive Oil, warmed
2	Small	Tomatoes, chopped and skinned
2	Medium	Mushrooms, chopped
1	Teaspoon	Mixed Herbs
2	Teaspoons	Lime Juice

1. Lay flat one of the sheets of filo pastry and brush with oil then now brush the other sheet with oil and place over the top of the other one.

2. Mix together the mushrooms, tomatoes, limejuice and herbs

3. Place the salmon in the middle of the sheets

4. Spread the mixture over the salmon.

5. Now draw up all the sides and squeeze the top together brush with the oil.

6. Transfer to an oiled baking sheet

7. Bake in a moderate oven at 375°F, 190°C or Gas Mark 5 for 12 to 18 minutes till golden brown.

Sausage Toad in the Hole

4	Thick	Beef Sausages
1	Cup	SR Flour White
1	Cup	Milk
2	Small	Eggs
2	Tablespoons	Vegetable Oil

1. Preheat oven at 425°F, 220°C or Gas Mark 7
2. In a bowl mix the flour, salt, egg and milk until smooth.
3. Use oil to grease two individual Yorkshire pudding tins.
4. Place a sausage in each tin and pick it well.
5. Put tins in oven for about 9 to 10 until the sausages are beginning to brown.
6. Remove from oven and pour over each sausage the batter mix return to the oven for about 20 to 25 minutes.
7. Serve with gravy, mashed potatoes and a green vegetable.

Three Cheeses Pizza

2	Cups	SR Flour White
4	Tablespoons	Extra Virgin Olive Oil
2	Tablespoons	Water
1	Teaspoon	Salt
1	Medium Tin	Tomatoes, chopped
4	Tablespoons	Mozzarella Cheese, grated
4	Tablespoons	Gouda Cheese, grated
4	Tablespoons	Edam Cheese, grated
2	Cups	Mushrooms, chopped
2	Teaspoons	Italian Seasoning

1. In a bowl mix the flour, salt, water and oil to a stiff dough.

2. Roll out the dough on a floured surface into a circle.

3. Then place onto a greased baking.

4. Heat a pan over moderate heat and add tomatoes and herbs bring to the boil and let boil for 5 to 7 minutes until the sauce has reduced by half.

5. Pour over base and top with mushrooms and the cheeses.

6. Bake in a moderate oven at 400°F, 200°C or Gas Mark 6 for 15 to 20 minutes till golden brown.

Turkey Curry

2	Medium	Skinless Turkey Breasts, cubed
2	Medium	Onions, chopped
4	Tablespoons	Butter
2	Cloves	Garlic, crushed
4	Tablespoons	Mild Curry Paste
4	Cups	Natural Yoghurt
2	Tablespoons	Coriander
2	Tablespoons	Sultanas
2	Teaspoons	Lime Juice
1	Pinch	Salt & Pepper

1. Heat a saucepan and melt the butter.
2. Add turkey, garlic and onions sauté for 10 to 15 minutes.
3. In a bowl mix together the curry paste, yoghurt, limejuice, coriander and sultanas.
4. Pour the yoghurt mixture over the turkey and heat gently for 1-2 minutes.
5. Serve with rice.

INDEX